PRAYING PROPHETIC PRAYERS

McDougal & Associates
Servants of Christ and Stewards of the
Mysteries of God

PRAYING PROPHETIC PRAYERS

by

Prophetess Jackie Harewood

PRAYING PROPHETIC PRAYERS

Published by:

McDougal & Associates
18896 Greenwell Springs Road
Greenwell Springs, LA 70739
www.thepublishedword.com

McDougal & Associates is dedicated to the spreading of the Gospel of Jesus Christ to as many people as possible in the shortest time possible.

ISBN 978-1-950398-52-2

Printed in the US, the UK and Australia and the UAE
For Worldwide Distribution

DEDICATION

I dedicate this book to the faithful pray-ers, intercessors, prayer warriors and special forces of the Lord of Hosts. There is a special mantel God has placed on the shoulders of those of you who stand in the gap.

ACKNOWLEDGMENTS

A special thank you to Prophetess Patricia Chambers, whom God used as a spiritual stenographer to record these prophetic prayers. Your faithfulness will be rewarded by God Almighty, El Shaddai, the God who is more than enough, more than sufficient. May He complete every promise of blessings and prosperity in your life. May He provide a surplus, a super-abundance, an overflowing, a good measure, a pressed-down, shaken-together, and running-over blessing for you! Thank you for your service to the Kingdom of God.

CONTENTS

Dear Reader,

At the end of each prayer, I have left a blank page where you might record your own prophetic prayer based on the truths of the Word of God and the truths which the Spirit, the Spirit of Truth, will reveal to you personally. Be bold to act on these truths, and you will not be disappointed with the results.

—*Jackie Harewood*

INTRODUCTION

At one point, we were impressed of the Holy Spirit to meet in our church on Saturdays to prepare the atmosphere for our services the following day. We did not just want to come together and say words. Rather, we wanted to speak prophetically by the Word of God and the anointing of the Holy Spirit, words that would move the heavens and shake the Earth. What follows are examples of the prayers we were led to dispatch from the earthly realm to affect the heavenly realm. The result was that we saw a great move of God.

Our decision to publish these prayers is with the hope that more of God's people will see the benefit of prophetic prayer. It is this author's hope that these prayers will guide you into a greater dimension of prayer in your own personal life and increase your knowledge base of the Word of God. May they stir the zeal of the Spirit in your own prayer life.

I urge you to be demonstrative and consistent in your prayers. The degree of your intensity in prayer will determine the level of victory that awaits you.

I can say without fear that God never disappoints. Although we sometimes fail to understand what He is doing, we can always know that He loves us, that He wants the very best for us, and that He is longing for a deeper relationship with us. This can be achieved, I am convinced, through *Praying Prophetic Prayers.*

Prophetess Jackie Harewood
Baton Rouge, Louisiana

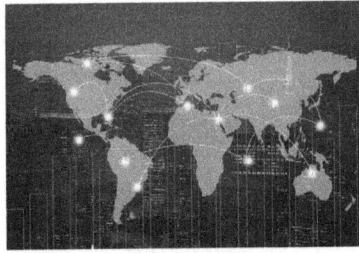

୨1ଏ

PRAYING FOR THE LOVED ONES WE WANT TO BE SAVED

Therefore seeing we have this ministry, as we have received mercy, we faint not; but have renounced the hidden things of dishonesty, not walking in craftiness, nor handling the word of God deceitfully; but by manifestation of the truth commending ourselves to every man's conscience in the sight of God. But if our gospel be hid, it is hid to them that are lost: in whom the god of this world hath blinded the minds of them which believe not, lest the light of the glorious gospel of Christ, who is the image of God, should shine unto them. For we preach not ourselves, but Christ Jesus the Lord; and ourselves your servants for Jesus' sake. 2 Corinthians 4:1-5

I cover them in the blood of Jesus Christ.

I break off every curse, in the name of Jesus.

The god of this world has blinded the mind of those who believe not.[1]

I command those blinders to fall off now in the name of Jesus.

I release them from the clutches of Satan and the influence of the world.

I pull them out of the fire by the power of the Holy Spirit.[2]

I command them to see in the name of Jesus.

Stop reasoning!

Stop making excuses!

I command you to come to the Light in Jesus' name.

Holy Spirit, convict and pull them out of sin, unholiness and unrighteousness.

Let them know that the way they are going is dangerous.

I pray that they turn away from sin and turn to You, Lord.

1. 2 Corinthians 4:4
2. Jude 1:23

I dispatch warrior angels, as our loved ones and others move through the passage on their way toward You.

I have a responsibility because we share DNA.

I command that part of our DNA to be sanctified.

I declare the DNA I share with them to be sanctified and holy, in the name of Jesus.

I declare that the DNA we share must line up because the part I share with them wants to serve God.

It is saved, and they are saved.

My salvation piece is already a part of them; it's already there in them.

My salvation is a part of their DNA.

They don't know it, but it's a part of their DNA.

It's in the strain—maybe an aunt, a cousin, a sister or brother,

Maybe a third or fourth cousin.

I decree that the strain I share with them is holy and sanctified.

Oh God, stir up hunger and thirst in them.

Stir up a desire to want everything You are.

You said, from our covenant with Abraham, that we share Abraham's DNA.

I spread it out to the aunts and the uncles, the first and second cousins—even by marriage.

I declare the blood of Jesus over their lives.

I thank You, God, for the revelation of the DNA!

I thank You for the revelation of our own DNA!

I give You honor, God! I bless Your name today!

YOUR PROPHETIC PRAYER TODAY

_____

_____

_____

_____

_____

_____

_____

_____

_____

_____

_____

_____

_____

_____

_____

_____

_____

_____

_____

_____

_____

_____

❧2❧

PRAYING FOR OUR NEEDS TO BE SUPPLIED

Bring ye all the tithes into the storehouse, that there may be meat in mine house, and prove me now herewith, saith the LORD of hosts, if I will not open you the windows of heaven, and pour you out a blessing, that there shall not be room enough to receive it. Malachi 3:10

Note: If you are a tither, God has already made provision for your needs. Just stand on the Word. Put a demand on the Word. Pull on the Word. God has promised to supply all your needs. If you give to missions, you qualify for God to take care of all your need according to His richest in Christ Jesus.

Give us this day our daily bread.

We ask You to give us the things we need for the daily operation of our homes and those of our families.

I declare that those in mission work stand under an open Heaven.

I am a tither. I stand on the Word. Therefore the gas in my vehicles lasts longer, and the tires on my car last longer.

The clothes I wear last longer.

My air-conditioner and washer and dryer last longer.

Everything I own lasts longer and is superb.

In Malachi 3, the Lord said He would rebuke the devourer from our money.[3]

I am a giver and a tither.

Thank You for blessing me with increase, increase in my job and business.

Bless me in my comings and my goings.

Lord, You will bless us when we invest in our thoughts because we are givers.

---

3. Malachi 3:11

Because I am to be blessing to the Kingdom of God, I invoke the Law of Reciprocity.

The more I give to Him, the more He gives back to me.

I know the secret:

The more I give to the Kingdom, the more comes back to me—in bargains, in transactions, in discounts, in contracts, in deals and in others giving to me.

I know the secret:

The more I sow, the more I receive.

The measure I mete out will be measured back to me.

If I sow little, I receive little.

But if I sow big, I receive a greater increase.

I reap what I sow.

If I sow bread, I reap bread.

If I sow strife, I reap strife.

I am not likely to reap money if I have not sown money.[4]

---

4. 2 Corinthians 9:6

Lord, give me this day my daily bread.

Father, do not give me just enough.

I confess that I have more than enough.

I have enough and some left over.

I ask, Lord, for witty inventions and business ideas.

I do not ask for just enough to get by because I need extra to help others.

Give me a strategy, Lord.

Give me a plan.

In the book of Acts, the believers in the early Church had more than enough.

And Your promises for today are the same.

I need to use wisdom.

I need a system.

Give me a system so that I can be of service to the Kingdom of God.

Thank You, God, for giving me my daily sustenance.

Help me to understand the principles found in the book of Acts.

The book of Acts is the precedence for the Body today.

What they did in Acts has to be our model. They brought their goods to the Church, and the apostles distributed them.[5]

5.Acts 4:35

YOUR PROPHETIC PRAYER TODAY

_____

_____

_____

_____

_____

_____

_____

_____

_____

_____

_____

_____

_____

_____

_____

_____

_____

_____

_____

_____

_____

PRAYING FORGIVENESS

Judge not, and ye shall not be judged: condemn not, and ye shall not be condemned: forgive, and ye shall be forgiven: give, and it shall be given unto you; good measure, pressed down, and shaken together, and running over, shall men give into your bosom. For with the same measure that ye mete withal it shall be measured to you again. Luke 6:37-38

Note: Be quiet and listen. Meditate on what God communicates to you right now. Living in the world, there will always be hurts from time to time. God has given us the strategy to overcome them. We are to forgive others as He forgives us.

I choose to forgive others that I might be
blessed.

In fact, I forgive others ahead of time.

I forgive them right now for the future.

I release those who will hurt me in the future,
just as I release those who have hurt me in
the past.

I forgive others as Jesus has forgiven me.

YOUR PROPHETIC PRAYER TODAY

_____

_____

_____

_____

_____

_____

_____

_____

_____

_____

_____

_____

_____

_____

_____

_____

_____

_____

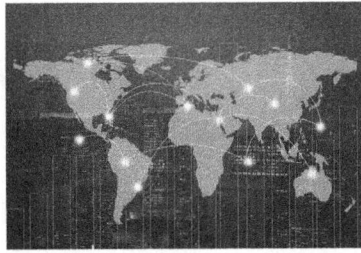

❧4❧

PRAYING FOR THE PERSECUTED CHURCH AND FOR SOULS

That the God of our Lord Jesus Christ, the Father of glory, may give unto you the spirit of wisdom and revelation in the knowledge of him: the eyes of your understanding being enlightened; that ye may know what is the hope of his calling, and what the riches of the glory of his inheritance in the saints, and what is the exceeding greatness of his power to us-ward who believe, according to the working of his mighty power, which he wrought in Christ, when he raised him from the dead, and set him at his own right hand in the heavenly places, far above all principality, and power, and might, and dominion, and every name that is named, not only in this world, but also in that which is to come: and hath put all things under his feet, and gave him to be the head over all things to the church, which is his body, the fulness of him that filleth all in all.

Ephesians 1:17-23

Father, I pray for those churches and ministries that have been persecuted and are being persecuted.

I lift them up globally.

Protect the persecuted Church.

I pray for India, South America, China, South Africa, West Africa, Pakistan ... that God would allow men and women who cross paths with sinners to witness.

I pray for the continents, the islands, for Germany, all of Europe, Iran, Iraq and Syria.

God, show Yourself strong that You may be glorified.

I pray for the nations of the 1040 Window.

Move there by Your Spirit, God.

Touch hearts, Lord.

I send the Word.

Protect the missiologists sent to serve along side the local nationals.

I pray for Bibles to be translated in their native languages and that the missiologists may be able to move in the native customs of each people group and have favor with the local nationals.

Have mercy on those nations, God!

YOUR PROPHETIC PRAYER TODAY

_____

_____

_____

_____

_____

_____

_____

_____

_____

_____

_____

_____

_____

_____

_____

_____

_____

_____

_____

_____

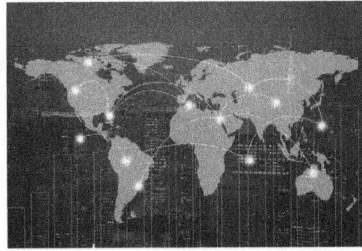

PRAYING FOR OUR NATION

Blessed is the nation whose God is the LORD; *and the people whom he hath chosen for his own inheritance.* Psalm 33:12

Let this nation be governed by the faith of its founding fathers.

I pray that government officials return to the fear of the Lord.

Move, oh God, that the people of this nation would rise up and stand upon the standard You have already set for the nation.

YOUR PROPHETIC PRAYER TODAY

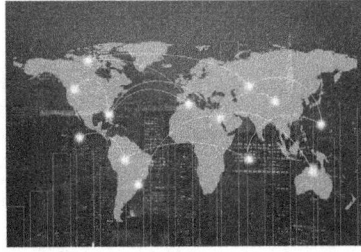

৯৹6৹৶

PRAYING FOR LOCAL GOVERNMENTS

I exhort therefore, that, first of all, supplications, prayers, intercessions, and giving of thanks, be made for all men; for kings, and for all that are in authority; that we may lead a quiet and peaceable life in all godliness and honesty. For this is good and acceptable in the sight of God our Saviour; who will have all men to be saved, and to come unto the knowledge of the truth. 1 Timothy 2:1-4

I life up my local and surrounding areas.
Take authority, Holy Spirit, over spirits of
    murder, anger, hatred and brutality.
I rise up against every ruling spirit in my
    neighborhood,

I rise up against bitterness, hopelessness and carelessness.

I rise up against pride and hedonism.

Satan, come out of our men in the name of Jesus.

I rise up against the same spirit in our women.

I speak life to them.

The spirit of death must leave.

Come out of their lives in the name of Jesus.

I speak hope, that they will see hope and live.

I speak hope into our neighborhoods.

I address the occupants of the neighborhoods.

Come out from among them and live.

I dispatch angels to bring them out from the east, west, north and south in the name of Jesus.

I command the enemy to loose the chains that keep you in bondage.

Thank You, Lord, for answering our prayer.

I pray for our city.

Spirit of the Lord, move as never before.

Father, they are coming from the north, south, east and west.

Spring up, oh wells, over this area.

Send out revival fire and burn up everything not like You, God.

Hallelujah to the Lamb of God!

You reign over all!

YOUR PROPHETIC PRAYER TODAY

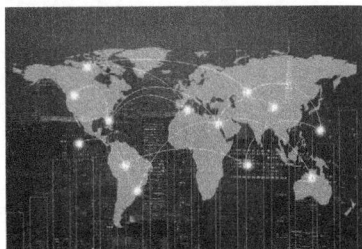

PRAYING FOR YOUNG PEOPLE AND YOUNG ADULTS

Let us therefore come boldly unto the throne of grace, that we may obtain mercy, and find grace to help in time of need. Hebrews 4:16

Let people turn their eyes to You, God.

Break every chain.

Raise up a standard of holiness and righteousness.

We come against every unclean spirit.

The devil is trying to hold the young people and young adults.

Show Yourself strong, Lord Sabaoth, in the community and the surrounding areas.

Spirit of the Lord, with eyes of faith I see souls being swept into the Kingdom of God.

Kingdom of God, move as never before.

Anointing of God, come down.

Let the Shekinah Glory of God come down.

Let Thy Kingdom come on Earth as it is in Heaven.

Thank You, Jehovah, for those who are called by Your name,

those who have turned from their wicked ways and are looking for a healing in our city and surrounding areas.

In the name of Jesus, I thank You in advance.

I thank You before it manifests.

YOUR PROPHETIC PRAYER TODAY

_____

_____

_____

_____

_____

_____

_____

_____

_____

_____

_____

_____

_____

_____

_____

_____

_____

_____

_____

_____

_____

_____

ఇ•8•ఌ

PRAYING FOR SUNDAY SERVICES

Let us draw near with a true heart in full assurance of faith, having our hearts sprinkled from an evil conscience, and our bodies washed with pure water. Let us hold fast the profession of our faith without wavering; (for he is faithful that promised;) and let us consider one another to provoke unto love and to good works: not forsaking the assembling of ourselves together, as the manner of some is; but exhorting one another: and so much the more, as ye see the day approaching.

Hebrews 10-22-25

I pray for a "Back to Church" Campaign.
I pray that our church will be flooded with the
   supernatural.

I pray that the Shekinah Glory of God will come and extend from east, west, north and south.

Let Your train fill the sanctuary.[6]

I pray that unbelievers from every walk of life would make decisions to serve Jesus.

Our nation has become a wilderness.

It is dry because of the affect of the sins of our time.

Let the fire of the Holy Ghost burn up everything that is not like You, God.

Burn up sin.

Burn up unrighteousness.

Release the love of God, the awesomeness of God, the power of God.

I pray for the love of God in our city and surrounding areas.

Someone is waking up, tired of their old lifestyle.

Draw them by Your Spirit.

Before the world changes, we have to change.

I believe You, God, for some new things.

And I am expecting to see them immediately—NOW!

---

6. Isaiah 6:1

I have been told to wait for "the sweet by and by."

But You, God, are a rewarder of those who diligently seek You.[7]

I believe You to do something right now.

I have "now faith."

Thank You for the service and a great outpouring of Your Spirit.

I will keep the wheel turning, the wheel of prayer.

Amen!

---

7. Hebrew 11:6

YOUR PROPHETIC PRAYER TODAY

_____

_____

_____

_____

_____

_____

_____

_____

_____

_____

_____

_____

_____

_____

_____

_____

_____

_____

_____

_____

_____

_____

ೂ9ೞ

PRAYING REVELATION 5

And they sung a new song, saying, Thou art worthy to take the book, and to open the seals thereof: for thou wast slain, and hast redeemed us to God by thy blood out of every kindred, and tongue, and people, and nation; and hast made us unto our God kings and priests: and we shall reign on the earth. And I beheld, and I heard the voice of many angels round about the throne and the beasts and the elders: and the number of them was ten thousand times ten thousand, and thousands of thousands; saying with a loud voice, Worthy is the Lamb that was slain to receive power, and riches, and wisdom, and strength, and honour, and glory, and blessing. And every creature which is in heaven, and on the earth, and under the earth, and such as are

*in the sea, and all that are in them, heard I saying,
Blessing, and honour, and glory, and power, be unto
him that sitteth upon the throne, and unto the Lamb
for ever and ever.*   Revelation 5:9-13

Worthy is the Lamb that was slain.

We join with the four and twenty elders.

We stand in the midst of the elders.

We thank You for our redemption.

We give You all the glory and all the honor.

All praise belongs to You.

We honor Your presence today.

We honor the Lamb and the seven horns,
    the seven Spirits of God.

We stand and recognize them, and we sing
    a new song.

You are worthy to break the seals and open
    the Book.

You have redeemed us out of every trouble.

We worship You forever.

You are the First and the Last.

You are great and mighty Master of the Universe,
    the soon-coming King.

We stand with the hosts of Heaven.

Even Heaven and Earth sing Your praises today.

Thank You for being our All-in-All.

With every creature in the sea, over and under, we bless Your presence.

We honor Your presence.

We esteem You today.

You are the Most Valuable One we care about.

We acknowledge You alone.

You are worthy and most treasured.

We give You all the honor, all the glory and all the praise.

All dignity belongs to You.

Glory to Your presence!

Glory to Your essence!

We give You the highest esteem, the greatest praise.

We can never experience anything greater than You.

Every Word You speak is great!

All power belongs to You.

All dominion belongs to You.

All might belongs to You.

And all strength belongs to You!

You are Elohim, the Many-Breasted One.

We look to You for our every need.

Jehovah, the Self-Existent One,Great is Your faithfulness.

We position ourselves as we enter into Your presence with thanksgiving.

We come by way of the blood.

Because of the blood, we have forgiveness for our sins—even former sins.

We declare the blood.

We have access.

We bring it to our address.

Not by goats, lambs or cows, but by the blood of our Savior, Jesus Christ.

Because of the blood, we can prostrate ourselves before You.

Because of the blood, we can cry out, "Abba, Father."

You are our Father and eternal King.

Our Father, the Celestial Father.

YOUR PROPHETIC PRAYER TODAY

~10~

GLORIFYING THE ANCIENT OF DAYS

*I beheld till the thrones were cast down, and the
Ancient of days did sit, whose garment was white
as snow, and the hair of his head like the pure
wool: his throne was like the fiery flame, and his
wheels as burning fire.* Daniel 7:9

You are our God, our Father today, the One
     who sits on the throne.
You call us kings and priests.
Yet, You are the eternal God,
     Jehovah, our God.
You are Emmanuel,
     Jesus, the Son of the Living God,
     Yeshua Hamashiach,
     the Precious One.

You are our God and soon-coming King,
    and we recognize You as Trinity,
    the Holy One,
    the Ancient of Days.

YOUR PROPHETIC PRAYER TODAY

_____

_____

_____

_____

_____

_____

_____

_____

_____

_____

_____

_____

_____

_____

_____

_____

_____

_____

_____

_____

_____

_____

❧11❧

RECOGNIZING THE HOLY SPIRIT

If ye love me, keep my commandments. And I will pray the Father, and he shall give you another Comforter, that he may abide with you for ever; even the Spirit of truth; whom the world cannot receive, because it seeth him not, neither knoweth him: but ye know him; for he dwelleth with you, and shall be in you.   John 14:15-17

He takes from God the Father and gives to us.
He prays through us.
He is the Spirit of Truth,
  our Companion today.
Come in and pray, Holy Spirit.
We see You, Holy Spirit, as our Partner.
We see You today as our Friend,
  a friend who will never leave us.

You make God a reality in our lives.

You make us in the image of Christ and give us our prayer language.

Holy Spirit, You are a separate One in the Godhead, yet You are One with God.

God directs us by Your leading and imparts to us through You what He plans for us.

You give us revelation and make the Word clear and plain.

I see you as the One who shows us and guides us.

You impart to us so that we are part of God's Kingdom.

Now visualize your connection with the Holy Spirit,
Who unites us with the Father.
The Holy Spirit lives within us.
We are arrested by the Holy Spirit.
See yourself with your hands up,
surrendering to the Holy Spirit,
the Spirit of Truth.

**Let's move further into the Spirit and speak
in tongues, praying in the Spirit.**
**See yourself leaning into the Holy Spirit,
totally surrendered,
totally yielded.**

We lift up our hearts to You.
We lift up our spirits to You.
We surrender.
No longer do we live, but the Spirit lives in us
and through us.
We are arrested by the Holy Spirit.

**Let us see ourselves with hands up, surren-
dering to the Holy Spirit.**
Today we surrender.
It is no longer us, but You.
We have ears open to You, Holy Spirit,
listening for Your direction and guidance.
We yield to the Holy Spirit of the Living God.
You help us with our prayers,
making them with right intentions,
making them a sweet essence poured out in
worship to Father God.

Now, as we are lifted up in worship, let us move to intercede.

And we cannot intercede without armor.

So we put on the helmet (the helmet of salvation) to cover our minds.

And we put on the breastplate of righteousness.

We declare that we are the righteousness of God in Christ Jesus.

We see the blood, and we come by the blood.

We put on the righteousness of Jesus.

As we look into the mirror of God,

we know that we could never (in ourselves) be good enough.

We come under the righteousness of Jesus, the righteousness of His shed blood.

We put on our robe of righteousness that has been washed in the blood.

It is shining with the blood of the Lamb.

And, because of it, we stand righteous and holy before God.

We stand under the covering of the blood.

We are righteous and holy.

We are pure.

We have on the helmet and the breastplate.

Now we gird our loins with truth to keep all parts together.

Our truth is the Word of God, every jot and tittle of it.

We gird ourselves in truth.

Truth is the Word, and it shall not pass away.

We gird our loins with truth today.

You are Jehovah, Lord, our Banner and we are all girded in Truth.

Everything we have learned is held together by truth.

Every vision, every thought, ever intent of the heart, every plan, and every strategy ... they are all a part of Your plan.

You have given them to us.

We hold up a memorial (for purpose, Ebenezer) to You.

Every stone, every memorial, all that has been done in the past can again be done in the now and in the future.

The apostolic doctrine, we stand on it.

We embrace truth.

We gird up our loins in truth, thinking on those things which are honest, lovely and whatever is of a good report.

We expel everything else that is not of You, God.

Your truth stands the test of time.

We trust in what You have done in the past.

We trust, not just *something* that is true.

We trust in THE TRUTH.

We let the Holy Spirit cleanse us of anything that may not be God's Truth, but may be our own truth.

Be sure to stand on God's truth alone.

Today, Holy Spirit, reinforce the truth that God has spoken,
  not just learned and acquired behavior patterns,
  not just ideas we've picked up along the way and now believe to be true,
  not quasi-truths about El Elohim.

Therefore, Holy Spirit, we repent.

We ask forgiveness and that we now be released
from those lies the enemy has told us,
those opinions we picked up from our
families,
those cultural ideas we held so dear.
Forgive us, cleanse us and release us from the
lies.
And pour out Your Truth, Father, over us.
We only want You.
We only want Your Truth.
So, help us.
We decree a "cease and desist order."
The devil knows about legality.
Sometimes our human spirit, our will, reacts
and is not in concert with Your Spirit.
Today we issue a "cease and desist order."
Help us, Lord, so that Your will is done,
and we are not hindered by the enemy.
It is the will of God.

YOUR PROPHETIC PRAYER TODAY

_____

_____

_____

_____

_____

_____

_____

_____

_____

_____

_____

_____

_____

_____

_____

_____

_____

_____

_____

_____

_____

_____

ॐ12ॐ

PRAYING IN TONGUES

For if I pray in an unknown tongue, my spirit prayeth, but my understanding is unfruitful. What is it then? I will pray with the spirit, and I will pray with the understanding also: I will sing with the spirit, and I will sing with the understanding also.

1 Corinthians 14:14-15

Speaking in tongues, praying in the Spirit, we can go before God's throne and ask Him to issue a "cease and desist order."
We want to be covered by His Truth.
We need to draw on our most holy faith, as we stand before the Judge of all Judges.
Dispatch angels.

Begin to lift up your most holy faith.

Your words should be different, not the everyday language, but a heavenly language.

Sounds from a new song, new diction, new sounds and syllables.

Be yielded!

Sing a new song!

I rebuke the spirit of hesitation,
the spirit of resistance.

I rebuke normalcy, in the name of Jesus!

I release the new sound, new syllables in tongues!

We don't want to leave this realm until new tongues come.

We want to go before the throne with new tongues.

It's not about volume.

It has to be new tongues.

Old things have passed away.

Find your holy tongue.

Build up your most holy faith.

Your mind may try to keep you down.

Don't worry about the *status quo* or how it is
    supposed to sound.
As we stand before the Ancient of Days,
    stand tall before the Lord.
He is giving us power.
Stand taller, taller than we've ever stood
    before.
You are now with the Judge of Judges.
You are well dressed in your most holy faith,
    Standing before Him, in His presence, be-
    fore His throne.
Angels surrender.
A position we've prayed for,
    a place we've sought,
    an event we've been waiting for ...
Keep talking to the Father now, close up and
    face-to-face,
    your spirit man standing strong,
    standing stronger.
Communicate with Him today.
Keep praying! Keep praying!
Ask Him to grant a "cease and desist" order
    against any plans against Faith City on
    Plank Road under the auspices of Apostle

David Harewood and Prophetess Jackie Harewood.

Here in the court, as one before the throne,
  we come covered by the blood.
Here, with our most holy faith,
  we have on the helmet of faith,
  our loins girded up to protect us
  individually and corporately.

We ask You, Lord, that You display kind-
  ness toward us at Faith City International
  Ministry.
Protect us with this order against the enemy
  from anything that might deviate from
  Your Truth.
We stand in Your Truth.
Still the hand of the enemy!

YOUR PROPHETIC PRAYER TODAY

_____

_____

_____

_____

_____

_____

_____

_____

_____

_____

_____

_____

_____

_____

_____

_____

_____

_____

_____

_____

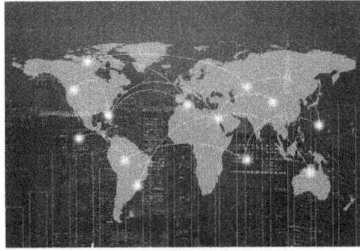

❦13❧

PRAYING REVELATION 4

After this I looked, and, behold, a door was opened in heaven: and the first voice which I heard was as it were of a trumpet talking with me; which said, Come up hither, and I will shew thee things which must be hereafter. And immediately I was in the spirit: and, behold, a throne was set in heaven, and one sat on the throne. And he that sat was to look upon like a jasper and a sardine stone: and there was a rainbow round about the throne, in sight like unto an emerald. And round about the throne were four and twenty seats: and upon the seats I saw four and twenty elders sitting, clothed in white raiment; and they had on their heads crowns of gold. And out of the throne proceeded lightnings and thunderings and voices:

*and there were seven lamps of fire burning before
the throne, which are the seven Spirits of God.*

Revelation 4:1-5

Now, just stand there.
Stand before the throne,
   covered in the blood of Jesus.
Our strength is through the blood.
He is making declarations on our behalf.
Stand strong.
He said He will issue that "cease and desist"
   order.
He will send angels to enforce it.
We must do nothing.
Thank God that we have that order.
Thank Him, and receive the order.
We give Jesus all the honor, all the glory.
Some things will change because of this order
   God has issued against the enemy for us.
We have gained a victory before His throne.

YOUR PROPHETIC PRAYER TODAY

∽14∾

PRAYING REVELATION 5:8

And when he had taken the book, the four beasts and four and twenty elders fell down before the Lamb, having every one of them harps, and golden vials full of odours, which are the prayers of saints. Revelation 5:8

Those prayer have gone to the throne room.
They are collected in a vial.
As we come close, we pray for the service
   Sunday,
     that God would visit us powerfully,
     that people in the city would become
   God-conscious.
Thank God for His goodness and mercy.

I pray not just for people's survival, but for their life in Christ.

We speak to the city and to the families today.

We break down walls and barriers and set the captives free from every barrier that has held them back.

We break down walls and see handcuffs falling off and shackles falling off.

No more excuses!

We see men getting free and serving Jesus.

We loose Your Spirit into this city.

Into Zachary, Baker, Clinton and all the surrounding areas.

We give You all the praise, glory and honor.

And we pray every word in the name of Jesus.

This is not the work of a man, but of the Living God.

We will see with our eyes and hear with our ears what God has to say.

We bless everyone—children, mothers, fathers, aunts, uncles

all families and church relationships.

Bless us on Sunday, Lord.

From this place, we declare healing to go forth
and restoration to flow.

May there be no feeble among us.

Thank You for doing it for us, Lord.

We thank You, Father, for what You are doing,
causing men and women to know Jesus.

No more excuses!

No more backslidden spirits!

No more stumbling about!

Get up! Get up!

Thank You for a great move of Your Spirit, like
no other.

And we give You all the praise, honor and
glory!

YOUR PROPHETIC PRAYER TODAY

_____

_____

_____

_____

_____

_____

_____

_____

_____

_____

_____

_____

_____

_____

_____

_____

_____

_____

_____

_____

_____

_____

_____

❧15❧

GIVING THANKS

In every thing give thanks: for this is the will of God in Christ Jesus concerning you.

1 Thessalonians 5:18

We thank You, Lord, for what You're going to do in the church, community, state and nation.

Thank You for allowing us to open our eyes because it is in You that we live and breath and have our being.

Thank You for protecting us.

We were able to rest in You.

Thank You for helping us to walk in purpose.

We stand firm in what You have given us to do.

One of the purposes is to win souls for Your
Kingdom.

We come standing in agreement to call back
those who don't know You,
those who have left You,
and those being mislead and misguided.

We call them back to You.

You are a loving Father and have all our best
interests at heart.

Thank You for repentant hearts,
as they come to You,
that they will repent.

And You will deliver them, heal them
and set them free in the name of Jesus.

YOUR PROPHETIC PRAYER TODAY

_____

_____

_____

_____

_____

_____

_____

_____

_____

_____

_____

_____

_____

_____

_____

_____

_____

_____

_____

_____

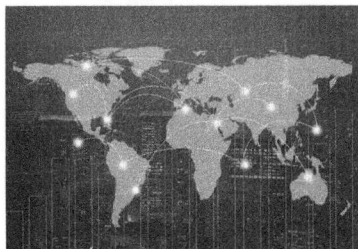

PETITIONING THE FATHER

And if we know that he hear us, whatsoever we ask, we know that we have the petitions that we desired of him.   1 John 5:15

Lord, we come petitioning You,
    that You would look down on Your children,
    Generations X, Y and Z and Alpha.
Touch them, Lord, as they prepare for school,
    going to their pick-up stations
    and as they enter into their classrooms.
They need those whom You send to encourage them, uplift them
    and lead them while they are young,
    positive role models and influences so they
    can grow up to be better men and women.

75

Give them good role models who know how to
  pray.
Thank You for their parents, Lord, who will not
    be led by others, but will seek godly counsel,
    those who know how to minister to the in-
    ner spirits,
    a place of ministry, not judgment.
Send those who would be able to release them
    from what's bothering them,
    the things that trouble them
    and the problems at home that worry them.
Let them know what it means to be loved.
We pray that the right person would cross their
    paths,
    someone who can see beyond the shell and
    see the real person,
    the one traumatized and hurting.
Thank You, God, that they have the Spirit of
    discernment.
They can see what needs to be done.
They can reach them and love them and cause
    them to open up,
    so we can get to the heart of the matter,

and we can get resources to them,
>so they can get the care they need.

You said You would supply all our needs.

We are mere guides and reinforcement.

Even in the natural, show them the way to go.

We come against fear (when people say they
>can't get involved because of the backlash,
>fear of being hurt or harmed).

We come against other hindrances.

We tear down walls of rejection,
>doubt and unbelief,
>the retaliation and the restrictions.

Send those who can assist those who need help.

Be the Bridge to Your people because the blood
>is the connecting line to You.

Some are at the crossroads of decisions,
>but they shall not go the way of death and
>destruction.

We pray that they go on the path that leads to
>You.

May their homes and shelters be safe havens
>for children.

Take them off the streets and give them
purpose.

Thank You!

Take them out of danger and through danger
so they have a testimony of how You
brought them out.

We thank You, Father, for a mind shift,
a shift for change,
a desire to want more from life,
to want You.

We pray positive role models find and influence the children and the adults.

YOUR PROPHETIC PRAYER TODAY

_____

_____

_____

_____

_____

_____

_____

_____

_____

_____

_____

_____

_____

_____

_____

_____

_____

_____

_____

_____

_____

_____

❦17❧

PRAYING FOR GOVERNMENT SYSTEMS

And the LORD spake unto Moses, saying, See, I have called by name Bezaleel the son of Uri, the son of Hur, of the tribe of Judah: and I have filled him with the spirit of God, in wisdom, and in understanding, and in knowledge, and in all manner of workmanship, to devise cunning works, to work in gold, and in silver, and in brass, and in cutting of stones, to set them, and in carving of timber, to work in all manner of workmanship. And I, behold, I have given with him Aholiab, the son of Ahisamach, of the tribe of Dan: and in the hearts of all that are wise hearted I have put wisdom, that they may make all that I have commanded thee; the tabernacle of the congregation, and the ark of the testimony, and the mercy seat that is thereupon, and all the furniture of the tabernacle, and the table and his furniture, and the pure candlestick with all his furniture, and the altar of incense, and the altar of burnt offering with all his furniture, and the laver and his foot, and the cloths of service, and the holy garments for Aaron the priest, and the garments of his sons, to minister in the priest's office, and the anointing oil, and sweet incense for the holy place: according to all that I have commanded thee shall they do.   Exodus 31:1-11

We speak to the systems of local, state and national government, staff officials and legislators.

Thank You for federal and state officials who will judge morally, ethically and responsibly,

not based on their personal agendas.

They will work for their country and govern righteously,

not for themselves, but from love,
not to make a name for themselves.
They will have caring, loving and sincere
hearts for a better community, state and
nation.
We know those in legislative positions want
to make righteous laws and be Kingdom
minded.
Those in authority will have a heart after You.
Let them be a voice for You
and let them speak as a mouthpiece for You,
Lord.
May they keep You in the forefront.
May they stand up against opposition and be
strong.
May they not cave in to unrighteous demands.

Thank You for doctors and lawyers and those
who do not care about being famous,
nor making a name for themselves.
Thank You for doctors and lawyers who de-
fend righteousness,
for judges filled with the Holy Ghost and fire,

those that have a relationship with You,
who will make a God decision for You and
Your people,
as they work in criminal justice.

Thank You for the military.
Thank You for the Armed Forces—the Air
Force, the Reserves, the Army, the Coast
Guard, the Navy, the Marines, the CIA and
the FBI.
Thank You that they will make righteous calls,
never purposely putting others in harm's
way.
They will hear You in the midst of attacks.
Bring them home safely,
these men and women.
Keep them safe.
Cover them and bring them home.
We glorify You and lift up the President and
his Cabinet.
Place righteous counsel around him.
Open his heart and ears to hear.
Give him a fear of You, Lord.

Touch him that he would be receptive to
sound advice.
Thank You for protecting him,
and may he give his life to You.
Your Word tells us to pray for those in authority and who have rule over us.
Bring revival.

Thank You for helping us to extend across
boundaries, from nation to nation.
Your Word is changing lives.
Thank You for missionaries, evangelists,
and those not afraid to go to the streets in
search of the lost,
for those who will pray and offer Jesus in
the store,
in the shopping center,
those who are not afraid to pass out tracts,
to get down in the trenches,
knowing they may be challenged,
and it might not be safe,
knowing they might have to take a few hits.
Bless them , Lord!

Thank You, Lord, for intercessors who know
how to go in and come out,
watchmen and gatekeepers who do not
sleep,
but stand guard at the gates
and who will say, "You cannot come in
here."
They stand with eagle eyes,
and will sound the alarm before anyone
else might see and say,
"This is coming," or "That is coming."
They call out for intercessors to pray the situation through prayer.
Let us have a hunger and thirst for prayer,
because everything is worked out through
prayer
and we can say, "It's already done," not
praying amiss.
We pray with a plan.
We pray with a purpose.
We pray with a strategy.
And we are already victorious.
We are already successful.

We already come out with the answers and
  solutions,
    with our hands lifted high and our mouths
    filled with praise.
We come out with adoration.
It's already done in the name of Jesus.
Favor has gone before us!
Goodness and favor follow.
We hold on to the horns of the altar,
    and we pray through and will not let go.

YOUR PROPHETIC PRAYER TODAY

_____

_____

_____

_____

_____

_____

_____

_____

_____

_____

_____

_____

_____

_____

_____

_____

_____

_____

_____

_____

_____

✍18✍

PRAYING FOR LEADERS

And he said unto them, The kings of the Gentiles exercise lordship over them; and they that exercise authority upon them are called benefactors. But ye shall not be so: but he that is greatest among you, let him be as the younger; and he that is chief, as he that doth serve.

Luke 22:25-26

Lord, we pray for leaders, as You show us
 what to pray for:
 for the people,
 for the praise and worship,
 for ushers and deacons
 for the fivefold ascension ministry.

We pray for officers of the church and for the altar workers.

We pray for church administrators, that You would show us what to do.

We pray that You would keep integrity in the House and integrity at the altar.

We pray that leaders will be righteous, not just looking for a paycheck,

that their hearts will be for souls,

for the people, not robbing and stealing from the people, but to minister love that will change hearts in the Kingdom.

May the leaders want to see change in the workplace,

change in the community,

change everywhere.

May they have excitement, and may You be their strength.

YOUR PROPHETIC PRAYER TODAY

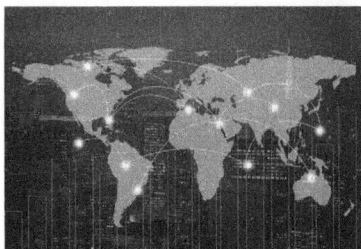

REJOICING IN GOD'S PEACE

These things I have spoken unto you, that in me ye might have peace. In the world ye shall have tribulation: but be of good cheer; I have overcome the world. John 16:33

Thank You, Lord, for peace.
With war all around us, we remain at peace.
The storm is all around us, but not in us.
"Peace be still!" we speak to the storm and the troubled waters.
This, too, shall pass.
Trials come to make us strong.
We draw strength from them.
They help to build us up in our most holy faith.

When obstacles come, we stand rooted and
  grounded in You,
  not tossed to and fro.
And, because we stand, people will inquire:
  "How did you do that with all that's going
  on?"
We will tell them, "It is by the grace of God,
  by our relationship with Jesus.
I draw my strength from Him, and therefore I
  am not moved by circumstances."
Many are the afflictions of the righteous,
  but the Lord delivers us out of them all.
This is the confidence we have because
  God is not a man that He should lie.
He is a Promise Keeper.
His every promise is "yes" and "amen!"
We stand on the Word of God. It is a shield to
  those who pray.
We are living epistles, not just inside of a
  church.
We are coming out so that others can also
  come out.

We are not in the church today and then the world tomorrow.

Then they would say that we are doing the same things they are doing.

Let us be beacons of light to draw them to You, Lord.

YOUR PROPHETIC PRAYER TODAY

_____

_____

_____

_____

_____

_____

_____

_____

_____

_____

_____

_____

_____

_____

_____

_____

_____

_____

_____

_____

_____

꩜20꩜

PRAYING FOR THE MEDIA

As cold waters to a thirsty soul, so is good news from a far country. Proverbs 25:25

We thank You for the media,
    but let them be changed for righteousness.
Programs on the radio, movies, the arts ...
    let God-fearing change arise.
Stop men from making inappropriate movies.
We call for a shift, a change.
We stand for righteousness.
Cause magazine editors and actors to stand
    up for righteousness in media.
The same for social media outlets: Instagram,
    Facebook, etc.

Your weight carries far greater than man's weight, not just about dollars, but to be a blessing.

Thank You for placing the right people in authority positions who will stand up and be a voice for righteousness in the popular media.

YOUR PROPHETIC PRAYER TODAY

_____

_____

_____

_____

_____

_____

_____

_____

_____

_____

_____

_____

_____

_____

_____

_____

_____

_____

_____

_____

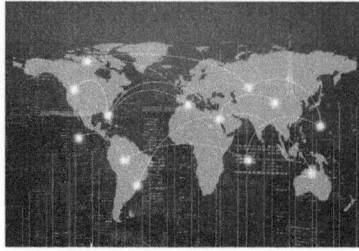

PRAYING FOR A TURNAROUND, A SHIFT IN ATTITUDES

They shall perish, but thou shalt endure: yea, all of them shall wax old like a garment; as a vesture shalt thou change them, and they shall be changed. Psalm 102:26

Lord, thank You for change and shifts away
    from generational curses and habits,
    what we saw our grandparents do
    and those who were caught up in religion.
Today they will be the change that produces a
    better life.
No more abusers, no more thieves, no more
    whoremongers,
No longer, in the name of Jesus!

Come out of religion and
   be free in your minds for change.
Thank You for the change,
   change for the better,
   change to positive positions in the Kingdom.
Thank You for pursuing our hearts.
You never quit seeking after us.
You open doors for us,
   and we open doors for others.
You are always making a way for us,
   and we receive Your ways.
Move on the hearts of Your people,
   so they are not just going to church
Thank You for the life change.
Thank You for leading us in the right way,
   to do Your will.
Thank You that they will come and "see a
   man"—the man, Jesus!
Like the woman at the well,
   they will meet You,
   and have an encounter with You.
And You will minister to their hearts.
You are the All-Knowing God.

Thank You for revealing Jesus to us.

They will come,

and it will be like a chain reaction,

a domino effect.

Change Your people, God, in Jesus' name.

YOUR PROPHETIC PRAYER TODAY

_____

_____

_____

_____

_____

_____

_____

_____

_____

_____

_____

_____

_____

_____

_____

_____

_____

_____

_____

_____

∾22∾

PRAYING FOR THE HOUSE TO BE FILLED

So that the priests could not stand to minister because of the cloud: for the glory of the LORD had filled the house of the LORD.   1 Kings 8:11

Lord, fill this house.
Keep them coming,
    so You can save them
    and fill them with the Holy Ghost.
We send strength now to the leaders who
    serve tirelessly,
    who hunger and thirst after You.
We lift Faith City International worship
    service,
    that people would come out,

and that You would take us deeper in worship.

That people would not come just to see a man, but come to meet You, Jesus!

We come to participate, not thinking about who is here.

And it's not about who brings the message.

We come to receive, but also to give.

Have your way, Father.

Thank You for the words going out today, for everyone pushing through together.

I pray a thousand-fold blessing, pressed down, continual growth, opened eyes, enlightened minds.

That they would forever give You glory and honor.

As You have said, the words of Your mouth will never return void, but will accomplish the thing they were sent to do.

We stand on Your Word.

We agree with Your Word.

We give You praise.

So be it, in the name of Jesus!

We bless You Lord!

In Christ's name we pray.

Amen!

YOUR PROPHETIC PRAYER TODAY

_____

_____

_____

_____

_____

_____

_____

_____

_____

_____

_____

_____

_____

_____

_____

_____

_____

_____

_____

_____

_____

23

PRAISING OUR CREATOR

Therefore the redeemed of the Lord shall return, and come with singing unto Zion; and everlasting joy shall be upon their head: they shall obtain gladness and joy; and sorrow and mourning shall flee away, even I, am he that comforteth you: who art thou, that thou shouldest be afraid of a man that shall die, and of the son of man which shall be made as grass; and forgettest the Lord thy maker, that hath stretched forth the heavens, and laid the foundations of the earth; and hast feared continually every day because of the fury of the oppressor, as if he were ready to destroy? and where is the fury of the oppressor?

Isaiah 51:11-13

We praise You, Elohim, our Creator,
Who has given us life and abilities.
You created us, and we honor You.
You are Elohim.
Thank You for making us to know who You
are.

Just think: He is Elohim.
Think about how He has made us.
Think about how He has made Himself
known to us.

Without You, we would just have existence.
We thank You, our Creator, Maker of Heaven
and Earth.
Thank You for power, might and strength.
Help us to rely on You to give us the strength
we need.
Continue to reveal Yourself to us.
We want to know You, not out of existence,
but as our Creator.
We make ourselves available to be known by
You, Elohim, our Lord God Creator.

Elohim, reveal Your plans and Your steps to
us.

Reveal to us what You are doing in the world.

Thank You for revelation today.

Give us clarity and insight and revelation, so
that we would understand these last days.

And, according to Your Word, let it be.

YOUR PROPHETIC PRAYER TODAY

_____

_____

_____

_____

_____

_____

_____

_____

_____

_____

_____

_____

_____

_____

_____

_____

_____

_____

_____

_____

24

PRAYING ISAIAH 41:1

Keep silence before me, O islands; and let the people renew their strength: let them come near; then let them speak: let us come near together to judgment. Isaiah 41:1

He is the One who has caused us to triumph. He is Elohim.

As you read Isaiah 41, remember Elohim, the Lord God our Creator and commune with Him.
In verses 9 and 10, He says:

Thou whom I have taken from the ends of the earth, and called thee from the chief men thereof, and said unto thee, Thou art my servant; I have chosen thee, and not cast thee away. Fear thou not; for I am with thee: be not dismayed; for I am thy God: I will strengthen thee; yea, I will help thee; yea, I will uphold thee with the right hand of my righteousness.

Thank You, Lord.

Do you see where our enemies will be?

Verses 11 through 13 continue:

Behold, all they that were incensed against thee shall be ashamed and confounded: they shall be as nothing; and they that strive with thee shall perish. Thou shalt seek them, and shalt not find them, even them that contended with thee: they that war against thee shall be as nothing, and as a thing of nought. For I the LORD thy God will hold thy right hand, saying unto thee, Fear not; I will help thee.

This is the Word of the Lord, and it continues:

Fear not, thou worm Jacob, and ye men of Israel; I will help thee, saith the LORD, and thy redeemer, the Holy One of Israel. Behold, I will make thee a new sharp threshing instrument having teeth: thou shalt thresh the mountains, and beat them small, and shalt make the hills as chaff. Thou shalt fan them, and the wind shall carry them away, and the whirlwind shall scatter them: and thou shalt rejoice in the LORD, and shalt glory in the Holy One of Israel. Verses 14-16

God will make us strong and mighty against our enemies. Not only that. He says the wind will carry our enemies away, and the whirlwind will scatter them. Praise the Lord!

As marvelous as this will be, we are not to rejoice over a fallen enemy. Rather, we are to rejoice in the Holy One of Israel, the Lord God Jehovah, our God, the Self-Existing One, Jehovah, Lord of All.

Verse 16 states the He is *Kadosh*, the Holy One of Israel. *Kadosh* means Holy Jehovah, our God, the Self-Existing One.

Lord, we see You as You are today,
    the Eternal One, the Holy One.
We are not just reading through scripture.
We are reading through the eyes of Kadosh,
    the Holy One.
These are His promises to you and me.

YOUR PROPHETIC PRAYER TODAY

_____

_____

_____

_____

_____

_____

_____

_____

_____

_____

_____

_____

_____

_____

_____

_____

_____

_____

_____

_____

_____

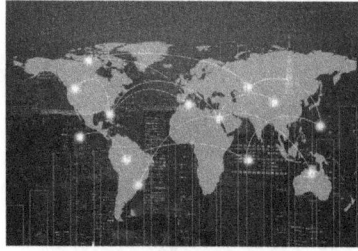

~25~

PRAYING AT THE BEGINNING OF THE JEWISH NEW YEAR

When the poor and needy seek water, and there is none, and their tongue faileth for thirst, I the LORD will hear them, I the God of Israel will not forsake them. I will open rivers in high places, and fountains in the midst of the valleys: I will make the wilderness a pool of water, and the dry land springs of water. I will plant in the wilderness the cedar, the shittah tree, and the myrtle, and the oil tree; I will set in the desert the fir tree, and the pine, and the box tree together: that they may see, and know, and consider, and understand together, that the hand of the LORD hath done this, and the Holy One of Israel hath created it. Isaiah 41:17-21

We prayed this from the vantage point of the
Jewish New Year.
This caused us to know that we would have
strength in the New Year,
a new perspective of Kadosh,
the Holy One, the Lifter of our Heads.

We have now put that into the atmosphere.
Let us embrace it for our lives.
Embrace it for the future,
and embrace it for today.
Let it sit a moment in your spirit.
Hallelujah!
God, You were here from the beginning.
You are Jehovah, the First and the Last.
You are Jehovah, the Self-Existing One.
You are Elohim, who calls generations from
the beginning,
the God of the Jewish nation,
God, our God.
You are the First.
You are the Ancient of Days.
You are theAlpha and Omega.

You are the great I Am,
>the all-encompassing God.

Thank You, God.

You called generations from the beginning.

You opened the Red Sea,
>causing us to pass through,
>and today You continue to keep us.

Glory to God!

The isles saw it, and feared; the ends of the earth were afraid, drew near, and came.   Verse 5

This relates to Jesus not being moved. It is a picture of salvation. He was fastened to the cross with nails.

But thou, Israel, art my servant, Jacob whom I have chosen, the seed of Abraham my friend.
                              Verse 8

The seed, spoken of in verse 8, refers to us, God's chosen people. We are now the seed of Abraham that God has chosen.

117

Let's stop for a minute and see the stages through the generations. The line went from Abraham, to Isaac, to Jacob. Abraham was a friend of God, and therefore God chose Abraham's descendents to be His people. Again, God said, *"But you, Israel, are My servant, Jacob, whom I have chosen."* From that point on, God brought His people through many difficult circumstances, and He kept doing it from generation to generation. Today, He continues to bring us out of all sorts of situations.

Life before Jesus was very different, but even then God was visibly with His people. Today, after all that Jesus has done for us on the cross, God is continuing to bring us out of every difficult situation.

Why? Because we are His chosen. Yes, He chose you and me. No matter how plain or seemingly ordinary we might be, He has chosen us and set us on high with Christ Jesus.

Thank You, God, for choosing us
Thank You for keeping us

118

Thank You for engrafting us into the tree.

Thank You that we are the seed of Abraham.

We have been adopted into the fold through faith in Your Word.

We are the righteousness of Christ by the blood of Jesus.

We enter in by the blood.

We are washed by the blood.

We take our righteous place.

We have been blessed with authority.

We are Your covenant people.

We proclaim the name of Jesus Christ.

We will receive our own property and deed it over to You, God.

We will redeem the land and stand on Your Word.

We rise up as a nation, the seed of Abraham, and bring redemption to the land.

We are blessed of God, and You give us good success, adding no sorrow.

We stand in oneness.

We stand in unity on the church land, bought by the blood,

redeemed by the blood of the Lamb,

because of our covenant as children of
 Abraham,

and because we proclaim Jesus.

YOUR PROPHETIC PRAYER TODAY

_____

_____

_____

_____

_____

_____

_____

_____

_____

_____

_____

_____

_____

_____

_____

_____

_____

_____

_____

_____

_____

_____

_____

_____

❧26❧

REDEEMING THE LAND

For I brought thee up out of the land of Egypt,
and redeemed thee out of the house of servants;
and I sent before thee Moses, Aaron, and Miriam.

Micah 6:4

We redeem the land You have given us
Our residences are a part of Abraham's
   covenant
Where our homes sit we declare for our King!
We are co-owners of the land.
We are righteousness to the land, not our own
   righteousness, but Yours.
We dedicate the land to You.
We deed the real estate to You.
There are more blessings than we can imagine!

And we embrace the blessings.

We are the seed of Abraham.

We are the engrafted vine.

This is all a part of our birthright in Christ,
Whom we proclaim today.

We are the spiritual seed of Abraham and
have been given insight to make a reality
our inheritance—businesses, deals, entre-
preneurial ventures.

There is a door, a portal, we need to be able to
enter.

God, You said You would give us revelations,
strategies and plans.

We are being given a way to access the land
and the blessings of the land.

In our own sphere, in our own particular area,
we are to mobilize.

**Ask God to give you open doors and free
access.**

**Ask Him to send angels, that minister to
those of us who are heirs of salvation,
angels to lead us to the right people,
angels to guard us and protect our goods,**

warring angels to ward off those who would war against us.

Lord, You dispatch the angels to show us and give us direction.

We pray an end-time move of the Spirit to connect us with the person God has sent for us.

Ask God to reveal the plan that will work.

In the name of Jesus!

YOUR PROPHETIC PRAYER TODAY

_____

_____

_____

_____

_____

_____

_____

_____

_____

_____

_____

_____

_____

_____

_____

_____

_____

_____

_____

_____

_____

೮ 27 ೪

PRAYING FOR DIRECTION

Trust in the LORD with all thine heart; and lean not unto thine own understanding.
In all thy ways acknowledge him, and he shall direct thy paths.   Proverbs 3:5-6

Write down any impressions, visions, or words God gives you. This is what we have prayed, and God is answering us. Listen and see what He is showing you. Let Him direct your thoughts.

We give our thoughts over to the will of God.
We have the mind of Christ!
Now, we direct our mind and embrace the mind of Christ.

I command my mind to make the connection, so that You, Holy Spirit, would help me to think on those things which are pure, honest, just and of good report.

Help us to think on these things.

The Lord says, "Ask Me, and I will show you things to come,"
So we ask You, Lord: Show us!

Now ask Him as you pray in tongues.

Lord, You said if we should ask Your counsel, You would give it to us.

We ask for Your counsel today.

You said in Your Word that we would know which way to go.

Tell us which way will prosper us.

We ask You today.

Let us know if the way we are going is a prosperous way or not.

We thank You, Lord!

YOUR PROPHETIC PRAYER TODAY

∽28∾

PRAYING THE SCRIPTURES FOR DIRECTION

There are several powerful scriptures that we can use in prayer to ask God for direction. For instance:

Numbers 27:21:

And he shall stand before Eleazar the priest, who shall ask counsel for him after the judgment of Urim before the LORD: at his word shall they go out, and at his word they shall come in, both he, and all the children of Israel with him, even all the congregation.

If the priests of that day could stand before God and receive the needed answers for God's people, then we can do the same today. They had the power of the Urim and Thumim, but we have the power of the name of Jesus and of the Holy Spirit that lives in us.

Another powerful scripture we can pray is Judges 18:5. The people of Dan selected five good men and sent them to the prist to inquire of the Lord:

And they said unto him, Ask counsel, we pray thee, of God, that we may know whether our way which we go shall be prosperous.

So, we can ask today, God, which path is the right one for us?
We stand before You today.
So we can know which way to go, that our way will also be prosperous.

We ask today, Lord,
Is the way we are going a prosperous one?
Is this a productive path?
Lead us in the path of success.

Am I in your perfect will or have I veered off into some other things that clouded my way?

You know Lord, for You, Holy Spirit are the Spirit of Truth

and I come by the Blood of the Lamb, by way of the covenant of Abraham as I am the seed of Abraham.

I look to You alone El Elohim, the Self Existent One, the Holy One of Israel

Thank you for showing us the right path, the righteous and prosperous way

Thank You for divine guidance, now receive that guidance as you spend time with the Holy One, Jehovah God

Recommendations: **Pray this prayer again (as often as you like) until something happens in your spirit about the answers you are seeking. Then write them down too.**

Now continue to pray in tongues.

Oh, God, Your will is so important.

We ask again: is the way we're going right?

Will it be prosperous?

Will it push us forward, Oh God?

I know that prosperous does not always mean
money.

Will going this way cause me to break out and
break forth?

Is the way we are going the right way?

YOUR PROPHETIC PRAYER TODAY

_____

_____

_____

_____

_____

_____

_____

_____

_____

_____

_____

_____

_____

_____

_____

_____

_____

_____

_____

_____

_____

LETTING THE HOLY SPIRIT SPEAK

Before you finish praying for guidance, read Judges 18:5 again. Know that it is God's will to show you whether the way you are going will cause you to go forward, to break forth, or it will it hold you back and prevent your blessing.

Now, just allow the Holy Spirit to speak to your heart.

Vow to obey all that He shows you.

Then, once you have heard from God, go in
   peace, knowing that He will bless your
   way.

YOUR PROPHETIC PRAYER TODAY

_____

_____

_____

_____

_____

_____

_____

_____

_____

_____

_____

_____

_____

_____

_____

_____

_____

_____

_____

_____

_____

~30~

READY TO ADVANCE

And they said, Arise, that we may go up against them: for we have seen the land, and, behold, it is very good: and are ye still? be not slothful to go, and to enter to possess the land.

Judges 18:9

When God has spoken, it is time to act.
Don't keep praying.
Start doing.
Come on, let us go up against them,
    for we have seen the land,
    and it is very good.
Aren't you going to do something?
Don't hesitate to go there and take it.
You heard that, right?

That the land is very good?

Now, pursue it.

Go!

Run into God!

Run into the land!

Get up now, and take possession of your land!

You are well able.

Go ahead!

Dispossess the enemies in the land!

Arise, run into God's promise!

We are servants of the Most High God!

We are sons of the Most High God!

This is the time to arise and run!

Go in and take souls for the Kingdom!

Our prayers have risen before God as a flavor, a scent, a sweet-smelling substance.

He is pleased.

Now it is time for us to arise,
time to take the land and possess it.

We have prayed.

Now it's time for action.

YOUR PROPHETIC PRAYER TODAY

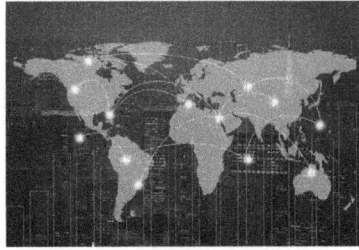

❧31❧

MOVING FORWARD IN FAITH

Now unto him that is able to do exceeding abundantly above all that we ask or think, according to the power that worketh in us, unto him be glory in the church by Christ Jesus throughout all ages, world without end. Amen. Ephesians 3:20-21

God, we know that in You we are able to do
  exceedingly abundantly above all we can
  ask or think according to the power that
  works in us.
Thank You for strength, Lord
Thank You for victory and enthronement.
Jesus sought me and brought me out.
He loved me and brought me into victory
We need His cleansing blood.

Thank You for ability.

Now all is done.

We have everything pertaining to life and godliness.

We are strong in You, God

We stand in power and cast down every imagination in our thoughts.

We are strong people who are triumphant because of You.

We are triumphant in our nation and land.

Give us new, supernatural strength and courage

Hallelujah!

We have put on truth.

Our feet are shod with the Gospel.

Hallelujah!

No weapon formed against us shall prosper, and every tongue that rises against us shall be condemned.

This is the heritage of the servants of the Lord.

We are secure in You.

Nothing is able to defeat us.

We are more than conquerors.

We are swift like an eagle, moving from an old
   mindset to a new one,
   being cleansed of all that is not like You.

And we are never going back.

We have our orders from the General,
   the Commander in Chief,
   the Lord Sabaoth.

We are on the move.

No more nonchalant spirit,
   for we are more than conquerors,
   always abounding in the work of the Lord.

We are stronger than when we started.

You have liberated us and given us hope,
   given us hope for the future.

We are going forward!

We are not going back.

Thank You, God for the lives touched across
   this city, community, state and nation

Your Spirit has wooed them,
   and they are coming out of dark places
   and into Your marvelous light.

YOUR PROPHETIC PRAYER TODAY

_____

_____

_____

_____

_____

_____

_____

_____

_____

_____

_____

_____

_____

_____

_____

_____

_____

_____

_____

_____

_____

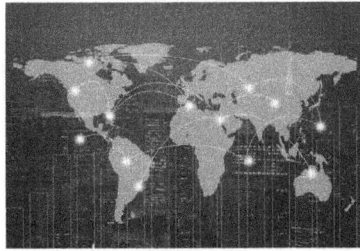

৽32৶

INTERCEDING FOR OUR SERVICES

*And this is life eternal, that they might know thee
the only true God, and Jesus Christ, whom thou
hast sent.*   John 17:3

We lift up our services, calling the people from
    the north, the south, the east, and the west.
We have sent out the invitation for them to
    come to this place to worship.
Now we pray that the Holy Spirit would draw
    them to come for such a time as this.
We pray now, Father, that You would draw
    them unto Jesus,
    unto the Holy Spirit,
    unto Faith City International,
    so that they can know the Word

and know they belong someplace special
   right here at Faith City.
When they hear the Word,
   cause them to make come alive.
We come against any distractions,
   anything that would impede the forward
   movement of the Word in their lives
We pray for every worker and for multitudes
   from every lifestyle.
This is not the work of a man,
   but of the Holy Ghost.

We have prayed and prayed, Lord.
Now show Yourself strong.
We come against every spirit not of God
   right now, in the name of Jesus!
Let blessings flow.
Let people leave saying, "This is truly a place
   where I understand the love of God."
Energize us afresh, God.
We renounce pride and selfishness.
This is a place of prayer, love and abundance.
Visit us like never before.

May You increase while we decrease.

Let this Spirit go around the entire world
and throughout the Body of Christ.

We are a praying people
of the Spirit of the Living God.

Move like never before
because we come lifting up Your name .

Let men and women come and see Jesus.

Let them come and understand who God is.

We give You glory and honor and praise,
Father.

**Now, let's give God all the praise, glory, and
honor.**

**A lot of prayer and footwork have gone
out.**

Now we expect people to come.

In the name of Jesus!

Hallelujah!

Praise the Lord!

YOUR PROPHETIC PRAYER TODAY

∽·33·∾

PRAYING TO OUR GOOD SHEPHERD

"Therefore, you shepherds, hear the word of the
LORD: as surely as I live, declares the Sovereign
LORD, because my flock lacks a shepherd and so
has been plundered and has become food for all the
wild animals, and because my shepherds did not
search for my flock but cared for themselves rather
than for my flock, therefore, you shepherds, hear
the word of the LORD: this is what the Sovereign
LORD says: I am against the shepherds and will
hold them accountable for my flock. I will remove
them from tending the flock so that the shepherds
can no longer feed themselves. I will rescue my
flock from their mouths, and it will no longer be
food for them."   Ezekiel 34:7-10, NIV

We have a Good Shepherd. His name is Jesus. Let's see Him as our Shepherd today.

Because men were not good and faithful shepherds of God's flock, He declared:

"For this is what the Sovereign LORD says: I myself will search for my sheep and look after them. As a shepherd looks after his scattered flock when he is with them, so will I look after my sheep. I will rescue them from all the places where they were scattered on a day of clouds and darkness. I will bring them out from the nations and gather them from the countries, and I will bring them into their own land. I will pasture them on the mountains of Israel, in the ravines and in all the settlements in the land. I will tend them in a good pasture, and the mountain heights of Israel will be their grazing land. There they will lie down in good grazing land, and there they will feed in a rich pasture on the mountains of Israel. I myself will tend my sheep and have them lie down, declares the Sovereign LORD. I will search for the lost and bring back the strays. I will bind up the

injured and strengthen the weak, but the sleek and the strong I will destroy. I will shepherd the flock with justice."   Ezekiel 34:11-16

He will search for His sheep.
He does search for His sheep.
We are witnesses of this truth.
We have been like the tribes of Israel, scattered.
But God has searched for us,
    brought us to Himself
    and brought us together as a people.
In this, He has revealed His greatness.
Just as He searched for you, when you had
    gone astray, He searches for others.
Stop judging them and love them as He loves
    them.
Just as you have felt the drawing of His pres-
    ence, they too will be drawn.
Verse 12 says:

As a shepherd looks after his scattered flock when He is with them, so will I look after my sheep.

Count on it, for He is faithful.
His promise continues:

*I will rescue them from all the places where they
are scattered, on a day of clouds and darkness.*

Clouds and darkness speaks of the circum-
  stances of life.
Zion is calling us to the High Place,
For we are the sheep of His pasture.
In verse 13, He declared:

*I will bring them out from the nations and gather
them from the countries, and I will bring them
into their own land. I will pasture them on the
mountains of Israel, in the ravines and in all the
settlements in the land.*

He is physically bringing His people back to
  Zion.
He is not physically bringing us back to that
  land, but He is drawing us by His Spirit.

We sense the pull of the Father, drawing us to
Himself, to His Heart.

We are gravitating to Him.

Zion is calling, "Come higher!"

I feel the pull right now in my heart.

Move toward the pull of the Shepherd.

He feeds us and cares for us.

The promise of verse 14 is:

I will tend them in a good pasture, and the mountain heights of Israel will be their grazing land. There they will lie down in good grazing land, and there they will feed in a rich pasture on the mountains of Israel.

I feel that gravity pull as He draws us,
and He is feeding us.

Today, Lord, we worship You and magnify
You.

You have connected us.

You have chosen us.

You have ordained us.
You draw us today,
 and we come as Spiritual Israel.
We come before Your throne.
We yield to You today.

Begin to pray and feel the connection, as He is pulling us.

We recognize that You have called us for such a time as this.
We recognize that You have led us beside the still waters, a place of restoration.
We are strong in Your strength.

YOUR PROPHETIC PRAYER TODAY

_____

_____

_____

_____

_____

_____

_____

_____

_____

_____

_____

_____

_____

_____

_____

_____

_____

_____

_____

_____

_____

_____

PRAYING THE 23RD PSALM

The LORD *is my shepherd, I lack nothing.*
  He makes me lie down in green pastures,
he leads me beside quiet waters,
  he refreshes my soul.
He guides me along the right paths
  for his name's sake.
 Even though I walk
  through the darkest valley,
I will fear no evil,
  for you are with me;
your rod and your staff,
  they comfort me.
You prepare a table before me
  in the presence of my enemies.
You anoint my head with oil;

my cup overflows.
Surely your goodness and love will follow me
    all the days of my life,
and I will dwell in the house of the LORD
    forever.   Psalm 23:1-6

We pray the 23rd Psalm because He is our
    Shepherd.
We are praying God's Word.
Our Shepherd has drawn us to Himself.
He searches for us.
Now, as we pray, we can visualize the truths
    of Psalm 23.

Lord, we really recognize You as our Shepherd.
You have sought us out.
We also see You as Teacher, Ruler, and the
    Herdsman who feeds the flocks,
    the One who takes care of us.
You are our greatest Friend today, and we are
    Your friend.
We are those who are grazing, for He has led
    us into green pastures.

Even today, You will take me to good grazing
 ground.

Oh my, I can feel the Shepherd.
Yes, He is the Self-Existent One.
Yes, He is my All-in-All,
 and my All-in-All is the Shepherd leading
 us.
Everything I need, He has given me.
He has allowed me to be His sheep,
 and He is my Shepherd.
David recognized that,
 and I recognize it today too.

Lord, I see You today as You tend the flock.
You have a one-on-one relationship with each
 individual sheep.
You are the One who causes me to go into
 good pastures
 and to receive everything pertaining to life
 and godliness.
It is all because You are my Shepherd.

He is a Shepherd that attends all His sheep.

He will lead us all in good pastures.

He is our Companion today.

He is entreating us today.

He is our Herdsman leading us.

Our souls rejoice today, not just our spirits.

The Lord is our Shepherd, and we shall not want.

He is our Shepherd today, and we have everything we need.

The Bible is not releasing us from Him as Lord, but He is also our Shepherd.

In our prayer time, we need to see as Ezekiel and David saw the sheep being drawn to Him. He went looking for us too.

We join the flock of Israel today.

We join them.

We yield our emotions, will and intellect to the Shepherd today.

We are seeking the God of all the Universe.

And He is our Great Shepherd.

He leads us beside still waters,
the still waters of peace and calm.
Pastures and meadows are for us too.
Our life is a pasture God has provided for us.

Thank You, Lord, for the pastures of our
homes, our dwelling places.
We sanctify our homes and those in them.

Yes, sanctify your pasture, your home, your
community.
You are there for a reason.
Pull on Acts 16:31, which says you and your
household shall be saved.
If we believe the Lord Jesus Christ, then
those in our household and those connected to us are saved.

We repent on behalf of the land,
the community,
for anything said or done not in keeping
with the Word of God.
We are godly tenants,
and this is a part of our abode.

We cannot rule over other people,
  but we declare that You have set good things
  aside for us.
We declare that You are Lord over our house.
We declare: You won all in our house.
It is Yours.
We recognize You as Ruler of the pasture,
  the green pastures,
  where everything is green,
  meaning there is growth.
The Church is growing and all those connected
    to it.
We see buds of life and sprouts.
We declare green pastures and new growth.
We speak life to our households,
  to the Church,
  to the community,
  to all individuals of Faith City International
  Ministry.
We prophesy to these grounds where we worship:
  Let life spring up!
We prophesy to the grounds where we live:
  Life, spring up!

Green grass is rising up!

Liberty is rising up!

Life is rising up!

God, we breath life today.

We speak life.

Let everything come to life!

We declare life for this church and this block.

This is the time for this block and this church to become green pastures.

Let there be green pastures where we work.

Let there be green pastures where our children work.

Let the generations to come walk and abide in green pastures!

You make us to lie down in green pastures.

This not only speaks of life, but also of alertness.

We ask that You lead us through dangerous places and any violence.

You supersede all violence.

You lead us to still waters, not disasters.

You rise up against violence, as we lie down beside the still waters.

We put on the helmet of salvation now for
warring against violence.

We put on the breastplate of righteousness
and the helmet of salvation.

Our feet are shod with the Gospel of peace.

We take up the shield of faith and the sword of
the Spirit, which is the Word of God.

So, we rise up, because we stand on God's
promise that He would cause us to walk
near still waters, not violent paths.

We rise up against danger and the spirit of
violence and anything that comes against
the Word of God.

We cast down every demonic presence in the
name of Jesus.

We hold up the Word of Psalms 23:3.

You can no longer aggravate and cause rifts in
the water,
like indifference in our households
and anger in the people.

We speak against every demonic force, and
loose and bind.

We crucify the works of the flesh
    and put them under subjection to the cross.
We nail all works of the flesh to the cross.
We nail every dark spirit on assignment.
We nail it to the cross!
We nail it to the cross in Jesus' name!

We not only bind it to the cross;
    we fasten it to the cross,
    the blood-stained cross.
The Word of God gives up power and author-
    ity to stop your work.
We operate in the spirit of judgment against
    you, Satan.
We rise up against murder and loss of life.
You must obey the Word.
We must walk in green pastures without
    disturbance.
We command you to drop your weapons and
    flee.
We loose you from your assignment first,
    then command you to leave.

We cast out murder, schizophrenia, mental
illness and selfish thoughts!

People of God, rise up!
Rise up!
Rise up in the name of Jesus!

You, demonic forces are operating illegally,
and we dispatch angels of war against
you.
We enter into a greater dimension
and cast them out.
We cast out bitterness and rebellion in the
name of Jesus!
We cast out the spirit of control in the name
of Jesus!
We cast out any possible retaliation.

**People of God, rise up, and cast it out in
the name of Jesus!**
Even devils and demons know the Word.

We command you to leave.

Spirit of jealousy, we cast you out
in the name of Jesus.

Now we are clean, and we cover those areas
with the blood of Jesus!

The area is now empty.

We now have to fill it with the Word.

In our workplace, in our church, in our homes,
let the Word of God reign supreme.

His Word is sharper than any two-edged
sword.

His Word will give us victory!

YOUR PROPHETIC PRAYER TODAY

_____

_____

_____

_____

_____

_____

_____

_____

_____

_____

_____

_____

_____

_____

_____

_____

_____

_____

_____

_____

_____

PRAYING AS ENFORCERS

*Let the high praises of God be in their mouth,
and a twoedged sword in their hand; to execute
vengeance upon the heathen, and punishments
upon the people.* Psalm 149:6-7

We give You the highest praise.
All praise, honor and glory is due to Your
  name.
We give the Lord a handclap of praise.
We reign victorious because we are equipped
  with the praises of God in our mouth.
We see the green grass.
Everything is new.
See the plants sprout.
See hope rising.

Good is rising.

Faith is sprouting.

God has sprinkled us with spiritual blessings.

They're coming into our house, our workplace, and our church.

Look back in the Spirit and see where He has
brought you from.

See hope!

See peace!

See an increase of love.

The table is spread abroad
to all those connected to us by faith.

We did not physically go to Israel,
but we have been with the Shepherd,
interceding and warring.

Today, we have enforced what He has already
accomplished.

Thank you, God, for how You've used us today in our meekness and humbleness.

Thank You for the green pastures,
for healing waters,
for restoring our souls,
for restoring our minds.

Joy is rising!

Nothing will separate us from this joy.

No circumstances gave us this joy.

Hallelujah! Thank You, Lord!

Thank You that we stand strong.

You give us entrance, and the Word is the door.

Thank You for coming in in such a mighty way.

Thank You for victory, abundance and touching lives.

Thank You for those who are coming.

Eyes have not seen,
    ears have not heard,
    neither has it entered into people's hearts
    the things which God has prepared for
    those who love Him.

We pray for the service tomorrow.

Thank You for moving greater than ever before.

We desire to serve You.

Faith City is a place of deliverance and healing.

Come and move in an awesome way.
Thank You, Lord.

Now just begin to thank Him
   for the ones seeking truth,
   the ones desperately looking for a place.

We come against everything that is coming
   against the people of God.
We declare a smooth flow in the house
   tomorrow
   and that they would come from the east,
   west, north and south.

Let's give Him praise.
One can chase a thousand.
Two can put ten thousand to flight.
We know there is more power in our unity.
We are looking for multitudes that can't be
   numbered coming into the Kingdom.
We pray as they enter.
We sanctify the grounds and declare them
   holy!

YOUR PROPHETIC PRAYER TODAY

_____

_____

_____

_____

_____

_____

_____

_____

_____

_____

_____

_____

_____

_____

_____

_____

_____

_____

_____

_____

_____

_____

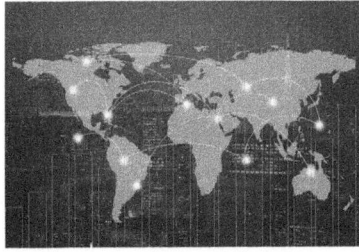

DECLARING THE BLOOD OF JESUS

For you know that it was not with perishable things such as silver or gold that you were redeemed from the empty way of life handed down to you from your ancestors, but with the precious blood of Christ, a lamb without blemish or defect. He was chosen before the creation of the world, but was revealed in these last times for your sake. Through him you believe in God, who raised him from the dead and glorified him, and so your faith and hope are in God.   1 Peter 1:18-21, NIV

We declare the blood of Jesus over this prayer
   time.
We stand and declare that it is not by bulls or
   goats,

but by the King of Kings
and Lord of Lords,
the Lamb that was slain.

His blood was shed to fulfill the Pentateuch,
  the Law of Moses,
  and to move us from the Law to Grace.
God, we thank You for the blood.
We recognize the blood.
Without the blood, there can be no remission
  of sin.
It is because of the blood that we are redeemed.
Old things have passed away.
We are under the New Covenant.
We are no longer controlled by the old man.
Today we acknowledge the blood.
We stretch out by faith.
We use our faith in this prayer time.
Reveal Your plan and purpose for us.
You said You would not do anything
  unless You first reveal it to Your servants,
  the prophets.

In this season, we are asking for Your interpre-
tation of Your Word,
for the interpretation belongs to the Lord.
We ask You to interpret Your Word and Your
will.
Because of the blood, we belong to You.
We belong to Your House.
Reveal Your plans to us, Lord.
We make ourselves available to You.

YOUR PROPHETIC PRAYER TODAY

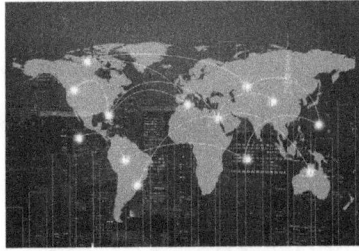

PRESENTING OURSELVES AS INTERCESSORS BEFORE THE FATHER

I urge, then, first of all, that petitions, prayers, intercession and thanksgiving be made for all people—for kings and all those in authority, that we may live peaceful and quiet lives in all godliness and holiness. This is good, and pleases God our Savior, who wants all people to be saved and to come to a knowledge of the truth. For there is one God and one mediator between God and mankind, the man Christ Jesus, who gave himself as a ransom for all people. This has now been witnessed to at the proper time. And for this purpose I was appointed a herald and an apostle—I am telling the truth, I am not lying—and a true and faithful teacher of the Gentiles. 1 Timothy 2:1-7, NIV

We present ourselves as those yielded to You,
as living and holy vessels in the service of
the Lord.
as intercessors that You can use us for Your
glory.
We are praying for Your interpretation.
We yield ourselves to the Holy Spirit,
to the Mediator.
God, reveal what You want You us to pray for
this day.

Now, listen!
**Hear what He says individually, but also
corporately.**
Intercessors, stand in the gap.
**Intercessors are bridges between what God
wants and the present conditions we see
that are contrary to His decrees.**
We stand in the gap for the nations.
We stand in the gap for every situation that is
contrary to the will of God.
We declare God's will to be manifested in
those areas.

We stand in the void, the chasm.

We have a spiritual anointing.

We are the access and the bridge.

We lay ourselves between the answer and the
   person,
   the city or the church,
   overlaying God's desire,
   His purpose,
   His plan.

You are a bridge because you have the answer.

You are the answer.

**We are the answer because we are connected
   to the One who has all the answers.**

We lay ourselves down in the middle.

We stand in You, God.

You cannot be manipulated.

We stand before You who holds the answer
   because we hold up Your Word.

We stand in agape love for the backslider.

He wants to come, but the door seems closed
   to him.

We form the bridge over which the backslider
can cross back over to Jesus.

So many things can prevent a person from
coming to the Lord,

so many things to divert their attention.

We move in rhythm today.

We are here to break the cycle.

We can pray them back.

We need to break the cycle of their rhythm, NOW!

El Kenai, a Jealous God, loves the backslider.

Still people cannot seem to come to Him.

We direct our attention from believing faith
to knowing that God is married to the
backslider.

You and I, we join God in loving the backslidden.

We rise up and break the cycle of the revolving
door over their lives.

We break that cycle in the name of Jesus.

We pray that the Holy Spirit brings each one of
them to a place of stability.

He will show you what keeps you in bondage.

Oh, taste and see that the Lord is good.

Proverbs 14:14 declares

The backslider in heart shall be filled with his own ways: and a good man shall be satisfied from himself. (NIV)

The backslider has a heart issue,
    a heart problem,
    but when the heart is fixed,
    he is more than willing to return to God.
Let us pray for the heart of the backslider.
Let's read it again:

The backslider in heart shall be filled with his own ways: and a good man shall be satisfied from himself. (NIV)

So, it's a heart condition.
The heart is filled up with one's own ways.
At one time this person was committed to the Lord.
But now they want what they want when they want it.

That's the revelation!
Whether they want money or a job,
   or a woman or a man,
   or to be popular,
   they want what they want.
That's the revelation.
Backsliders want to be controlled by their
   own desires.
I do what I want to do,
   when I want to do it,
   how and why I want to do it.
Whatever feels good is good for me.
They are comfortable.
They do not allow their hearts to be filled
   with what the Holy Spirit wants.
They substitute their own desires,
   and their heart starts leaning further and
   further from God.

A man of God once said he knew that something within him kept him from fully
   committing to God.
It was grounded in what's comfortable,
   what's easier.

It boils down to procrastination,
      not wanting to submit to the will of God
      because of one's own desires.
But today, we come against that spirit.
They need something to press them.
They need to be jolted out of that place.
We rise up and move whatever is in the way
      OUT OF THE WAY
      in the name of Jesus
This is our hearts' cry.
We cry out today for healing of the heart,
      that the backslidden would hunger after
      righteousness,
that the Holy Spirit would prompt the heart of
      the backslidden,
      in the name of Jesus.
All hearts that have grown cold, we declare
      that a fire should erupt and burn in your
      minds and hearts.
Burn up all that is not like Jesus.
Oh, God, let their hearts be turned back to
      You!
Let Your promises come alive in their hearts.

May they remember Proverbs 14:14 and push
their own ways out of their hearts.

Turn hearts toward You, Lord.

Some hearts are not totally gone from You,
but their love of You has been dampened
as they did their own thing.

Give the backslidden a new fervency of heart,
Jesus.

Draw them to Yourself!

YOUR PROPHETIC PRAYER TODAY

_____

_____

_____

_____

_____

_____

_____

_____

_____

_____

_____

_____

_____

_____

_____

_____

_____

_____

_____

_____

CALLING THE PEOPLE OF GOD
BACK TO THE CHURCH

Go and proclaim these words toward the north, and say, Return, thou backsliding Israel, saith the LORD; and I will not cause mine anger to fall upon you: for I am merciful, saith the LORD, and I will not keep anger for ever.
Return, ye backsliding children, and I will heal your backslidings. Behold, we come unto thee; for thou art the LORD our God.

Jeremiah 3:12 and 22

We declare that you are set on fire by the Holy
    Spirit.
You might not be on fire now, but we declare
    it to be so in the name of Jesus.

184

We pray for each to come back to the Church.

Only the Holy Spirit can convict of sin.

Holy Spirit, convict them of sin, righteousness, and judgment to come.

Make each one sin conscious.

Holy Spirit, touch their lives.

Bring them into alignment with God's will, so that we are not praying amiss.

It is the Holy Spirit who draws.

It is the Holy Spirit who convicts.

We pray for their vision.

Without hope, how shall it come alive?

With dreams dry, and fire only embers, nearly extinguished.

We pray for fire to light up their hearts.

We pray for hearts to FIRE UP!

The Word of God says that He is the one to help them.

The book of John tells us all the things the Holy Spirit does.

Holy Spirit, touch their lives and turn them back.

Help then to know Your presence.

Some have sat in the congregation.

Some have known Your healing power.

They have tasted and seen Your goodness.

Holy Spirit, draw them to repentance and restoration.

YOUR PROPHETIC PRAYER TODAY

39

PRAYING JOHN 16:4-5

I have told you this, so that when their time comes you will remember that I warned you about them. I did not tell you this from the beginning because I was with you, but now I am going to him who sent me. (NIV)

Since Jesus departed from the Earth, we have
the Holy Spirit,
and the Holy Spirit can help us in every
way,
even in our prayers.
We need the backslidden who have moved
into the world to come out of this world.
They have known life in the congregation.
Now they are listening to worldly songs

and are being seduced and influenced by the world.

Holy Spirit, You said You would reprove them.

We pray that the strength of the world will decrease and diminish in their lives,

in this season.

and they will return

to the House of the Lord.

We declare that the clutches of the enemy are loosed from them,

in Jesus' name,

and that their minds are no longer mesmerized by a substitute presence of movies, video games, music, which have claimed so many,

lulling them to sleep.

We say, "WAKE UP!"

We are the answer to someone's freedom today.

Those fallen into the New Age love of the spirit of Baal,

of false responsibility,

responsibility that God has not placed you
  in,
we rise up against the spirit of Baal.
You have armor on.
Now stand on the Word.
Stand for Truth!
Stand for God!
Be restored to His House!

YOUR PROPHETIC PRAYER TODAY

_____

_____

_____

_____

_____

_____

_____

_____

_____

_____

_____

_____

_____

_____

_____

_____

_____

_____

_____

_____

_____

40

PRAYING JOHN 16:7-11

But very truly I tell you, it is for your good that I am going away. Unless I go away, the Advocate will not come to you; but if I go, I will send him to you. When he comes, he will prove the world to be in the wrong about sin and righteousness and judgment: about sin, because people do not believe in me; about righteousness, because I am going to the Father, where you can see me no longer; and about judgment, because the prince of this world now stands condemned.   John 16:7-11, NIV

Be used of the Lord.
For the Comforter has come,
> **and He is reproving those who have backslidden.**

WE RISE UP!

We walk in victory!

We walk in Christ!

Gird up your loins!

Have your feet shod!

Walk in peace!

Hold up the shield of faith,
   believing the Word of God!

We see ourselves as a sword,
   extending from the hand of the Lord,
   the Lord Sabaoth.

We see ourselves as traveling through nations,
   atmospheres and times
   to every backslidden person.

If they are not on fire,
   if they are not fervent,
   then we refute their words,
   admonish and rebuke them
   in the name of Jesus

Rebuke them for sin and unrighteousness,
   for being lined up with the world
    and not with God.

The enemy has lied to them,
  causing them to step out into the grey area.
You are an extension of God today.
Speak into their spirits of the judgment to
  come.
Go beyond the outside and touch the inner
  man.
Through God's Spirit, we can convict them
  of every excuse.
Say, "I reprove them in the name of Jesus,
  and I convince them to serve the Lord
  today."
You are now praying spirit to Spirit.
"Come out of the world NOW!
"Come out NOW, in the name of Jesus
  and into the cosmos,
    the orderly arrangement God has placed
    you in."
I BELIEVE!
I see blind eyes opening.
I see an awakening,
  a waking up.
Slumber is leaving their eyes.

We win!

Now, Get them!

The captives are being set free.

People are feeling the effects of these prayers.

Every whisper God hears.

He says, "I will fill you up with good things,
   so open your mouth.
   Even the groanings the Spirit of the Lord
   gives is dynamic, giving life.

YOUR PROPHETIC PRAYER TODAY

_____

_____

_____

_____

_____

_____

_____

_____

_____

_____

_____

_____

_____

_____

_____

_____

_____

_____

_____

_____

_____

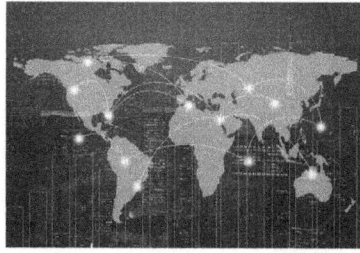

❦41❧

PRAYING FOR DELIVERANCE

Moses answered the people, "Do not be afraid. Stand firm and you will see the deliverance the LORD *will bring you today. The Egyptians you see today you will never see again."*

Exodus 14:13, NIV

We command all things not of God to be loosed off the people of God.

We command you to release your hold on the people you are holding hostage.

We denounce every power of darkness and every demonic spirit.

God's Spirit is the Spirit of Truth, and any other spirit is not of God.

We denounce you.

We call on the name of the Lord for our friends, our families and our neighbors!

God, touch their hearts.

Give us a door of utterance.

Spread goodness and mercy in their paths.

This place is a House of Prayer.

As we pray the for nations and for Baton Rouge, we break every stronghold,
every stoppage,
every blockage holding the people for centuries.

We come against it in Jesus' name!

We speak freedom in the minds, bodies, and spirits to serve God. A freedom from this Church, because as we leave free, freedom takes over and will reign in our hearts, minds and souls.

Any sickness ... we speak deliverance from it.

Heal those, deliver them from aches and pains and from every foul spirit of doubt and unbelief.

I pray for the anointing.

Every yoke is broken.

A yoke hold things together.

God says the yoke is cut off because it gives people the wrong direction.

We need the direction and guidance to serve God.

He is calling you and me to do that.

Freedom is in the house.

Whom the Son has set free is free indeed.

If you know it, raise you hands and shout!

Boldly speak out the words, "I AM FREE!"

We come against every demonic spirit and every human spirit and every spirit of doubt and unbelief.

I loose the holiness and righteousness of God. Thank You, God, for grace, for the peace of God, the love of God.

I speak general to general.

I declare this is a place where men and women come to salvation and deliverance.

Salvation is a change.

Deliverance is a change.

Let change come.

YOUR PROPHETIC PRAYER TODAY

～42～

PRAYING FOR CHANGE

Now arise, LORD God, and come to your resting place,

   you and the ark of your might.
May your priests, LORD God, be clothed with salvation,

   may your faithful people rejoice in your goodness.   2 Chronicles 6:41, NIV

When it comes to the Lord, I surrender.
I conform to what God has already decreed.
Thank God for Oneness,
   for the Holy Spirit,
   for the anointing.
We will extend salvation to others as never
   before.

We declare a spirit of excitement tomorrow.

This is a place where needs are met.

We see the glory coming and people getting a
word from the Lord.

We pray that people decide to come to Faith
City International,
that people just driving up and down will
decide to come in where their burdens can
be lifted,
where their hearts and minds can tune into
the Word of the Lord.

Even those walking the nearby streets will dis-
cover that something is going to happen as
they walk.

They will hear a new song, and it will go into
their spirit.

We pray that when they pass, they will come
in.

They will feel welcomed and know they are
loved.

We speak these things today.

God will take it from there,
moving on them.

And we thank Him.

Lord, do tomorrow as You like with the praise
team,
with the ushers,
with all the leaders,
with all the ministries.

Let this place be a place where holiness and
righteousness reign.

Speak to the hearts of hundreds and thousands of those crying out,
looking for a way.

Holy Spirit, woo them.

They will find comfort for their souls.

We glorify You today, Father.

Thank You, Jesus.

Praise the Lord!

Hallelujah!

YOUR PROPHETIC PRAYER TODAY

_____

_____

_____

_____

_____

_____

_____

_____

_____

_____

_____

_____

_____

_____

_____

_____

_____

_____

_____

_____

PRAYING WITH THANKSGIVING

Do not be anxious about anything, but in every situation, by prayer and petition, with thanksgiving, present your requests to God.

Philippians 4:6

Thank You, Lord, for all or Your Word and for
    every application of it.
Thank You for revealing Yourself to us.
Refresh us, oh Lord.
Prepare us for what is to happen next.
This is the Lord's Day.
We come prepared to serve You,
    to magnify Your holy name.
We call on You.
You are the God Who answers prayers.

Thank You that we have come to know Jesus.

Thank You for the Holy Spirit.

Thank You for all You have done in our lives.

We pray that every utterance is pleasing to
You.

We desire to open our mouths boldly,
to proclaim Your Word.

We can rely on You.

You are in our corner,
as we stand in the gap for others.

Give us strength to stand.

Make it easy for us to lay down our lives, Lord.

Touch our minds, spirits, and bodies
and strengthen all of our limbs.

We rebuke and cast out every weakness,
so that we will be able to stand.

We rebuke sickness and disease,
in the name of Jesus.

Nothing will hold us back.

As never before, we lift up our hands.

We are in our right mind
when so many others are losing theirs.

Thank You for all Your goodness and mercy.

You are our peace and our hope.

You are a present help in our time of need.

You lift up the Church.

Without You, we would be adrift.

Father, move by Your Spirit.

Thank You for lifting us up,
> for putting the right things in place like never before.

You are high and lifted up,
> and Your train fills this place and fills our lives.

Thank You now for making us the ones that make a difference in the lives of others in the different places You call us to serve.

Thank You, as we break down walls,
> as we loose the bands of the enemy.

This is the day the Lord has made, and we will rejoice and be glad in it.

Have your way, Holy Spirit.

Touch our community in a special way.

Deliver and heal us,
> for without You, we will surely fail.

I pray especially this hour

that You would change Baton Rouge to a peaceful place.

Thank You, Father, for allowing us to come to You.

We pull down strongholds,
in the name of Jesus.

We pull down all demonic forces that come against the people of God.

Holy Spirit, come in and do Your work.

Have Your way.

We give You glory and honor.

God, come in and touch the leaders of the Church.

Bless them and meet their every need.

You are our strength and our hope.

Touch now those who need finances,
those who need spiritual help.

You are able to do it, according to Your riches in glory.

You are able to do great things.

Touch those who need healing,
those who are sick.

Breathe upon us, Holy Spirit.

Lord, touch the saints.

Let revival break out.

Thank You for all the saints You are saving.

Do a powerful work in our day, Lord.

We pull down the strongholds of hate and prejudice.

There is so much havoc being caused in this area, but You are doing great things.

I pray for peace, that men come and bow to the Head Shepherd, Jesus,
and whosoever calls on the name of the Lord shall have life.

You came for this purpose.

Holy Spirit, let us be Your voice in our communities, state and nation.

Let everything and everyone bow down to Jesus.

Touch the saints in their areas of weakness.

You are a Way-Maker, a Heart-Fixer and a Mind-Regulator.

Do all things for Your glory.

We have strength in the midst of the trouble.

Today we pray for all that know Jesus,

that they all advance in the things of God
like never before.

We pray for change.

We pray for those in authority.

We pray for the Governor of the state,
the Mayor of the city and those who work
beside them, making laws and decisions.

We have a right to rule, and the people shall
rejoice.

We pray for revival.

Touch every member of the church,
every well-wisher and guest.

We pray for blessing and riches that add no
sorrow.

We pray that You will bless,
breaking every yoke
and anointing the people of God.

We pray for the power of the Holy Spirit.

Give us power and strength,
for we have put on the whole armor.

We come, not against flesh and blood,
but against spiritual wickedness.

Make us strong to do great exploits,

to look into the face of the enemy
and move forward with boldness.
Thank You for strength today.
We come against sickness,
in the name of Jesus,
and declare divine health and strength
so that we may do the will of God.

YOUR PROPHETIC PRAYER TODAY

_____

_____

_____

_____

_____

_____

_____

_____

_____

_____

_____

_____

_____

_____

_____

_____

_____

_____

_____

_____

_____

_____

∾44∾

PRAYING FOR STRENGTH

Do not be anxious about anything, but in every situation, by prayer and petition, with thanksgiving, present your requests to God.

Isaiah 40:29, NIV

We pray for strength in the face of the enemy.
We stand strong, having done all we can.
We stand with our feet shod with the Gospel
   of peace.
We say, "Lord, help Your people.
Purify us and give us aid from on high.
Dispatch Your angels to assist us in our time
   of need.
Our hope and trust lie in You, Lord Sabaoth.
Thank You for helping our mind, spirit and

body.

Thank You for the privilege to use the authority in Your name."

We pray that men and women, boys and girls come from the north, south, east and west.

I pray for the hearts of the people.

Holy Spirit, speak to their spirits.

Speak to their spirits.

Remove stubbornness from their hearts.

Let them hear when You call.

Give them the ability to respond.

We come against the plans of the enemy to cut short the lives of the people.

We command the spirit of murder to leave the territory now, in Jesus' name.

We loose the Spirit of Salvation in the atmosphere.

Lord, create hunger in the hearts of the people.

Except You draw them, they cannot come.

I command the god of this world to loose the blinders he has placed on the minds of the people.

I command the blinders to fall, letting the light of the Gospel shine in their mind.

Holy Spirit, convict men of sin, righteousness and judgment to come.

I ask You, Lord, to change the course of the lives of the people.

Send laborers into Your harvest.

Save the lost from a Christ-less eternity.

God, You said that Your wish is that none would perish.

Send a spirit of repentance to rest on the lives of those who are at a point of decision.

We read of revival in certain areas in days of old.

And we know that You are no respecter of persons.

I ask you to send the rain of revival.

Let revival flow from Your throne.

Let us be sensitive to hear the sound of Your revival and respond.

We see a special change coming,
a great change in our city, state and also our nation.

There are multitudes in the valley of decision.

Have Your way, Father.

Let folk be swept into Your Kingdom.

Let each one put his hand to the plow and not look back, Lord.

May we look to Jesus.

Help comes from the Lord.

Strengthen Your Church, Father.

And may we be that person who is a great encourager.

Let our lives be strong examples of Jesus because You have made us strong.

We pray to have the spirit of Esther, a for-such-a-time-as-this spirit.

We pray for souls to be saved and to come to know Jesus.

We stand strong and take the Spirit with us to bring them into new life.

We ask that You place a hunger and thirst in their hearts.

We know that they that hunger and thirst for righteousness shall be filled.

I dispatch the gathering angels to go and

gather those whom God has called to His Kingdom.

Bring them, plant them and establish them here at Faith City International.

I hear the angels rejoicing when sinners come to salvation.

I rejoice in advance with the angels.

And now we announce to the heavens that God is our Salvation.

YOUR PROPHETIC PRAYER TODAY

_____

_____

_____

_____

_____

_____

_____

_____

_____

_____

_____

_____

_____

_____

_____

_____

_____

_____

_____

_____

OTHER BOOKS
BY
PROPHETESS JACKIE HAREWOOD

Sing Unto the Lord a New Song: An Introduction to Praise and Worship
(0-97-9712623-0-6)

The Violent Take It by Force
(978-1-934769-11-9)

Intercession Builds Bridges: Frequently Asked Questions About Intercession
(978-1-59872-909-2)

Overshadowed by the Almighty
(978-1-934769-99-7)

Ballistic Apostolic Prayer
(978-1-940461-55-7)

Learning to Use Your Greatest Weapon
(978-1-940461-56-4)

Warring with the Scriptures
(978-1-940461-73-1)

Make a Joyful Noise
(978-1-940461-74-8)

Generational Curses and How to Be Free from Them
(978-1-940461-79-3)

The Violent Take it by Force

Force

Intercession Made Easy

Jackie Harewood

Overshadowed
by the Almighty

Understanding the Phenomeno[n] Known as "Being Slain in the Spirit"

With a special chapter entitled What Does God's Voice Sound Like?

Prophetess Jackie Harewood

Ballistic Apostolic Prayer

Jackie Harewood

Learning to Use Your Greatest Weapon

Prophetess Jackie Harewood

WARRING
with
the
SCRIPTURES

Arm Yourself with
Power-Packed Words to
Reign in Victory

Prophetess Jackie Harewood

MAKE A JOYFUL NOISE

An Introduction to Praise and Worship

JESUS

Prophetess
Jackie
Harewood

GENERATIONAL
CURSES
AND HOW TO BE FREE FROM THEM

Prophetess Jackie Harewood

I Will Bless Bless THEE

Discovering the Untapped Power of COVENANT

Apostle David Harewood

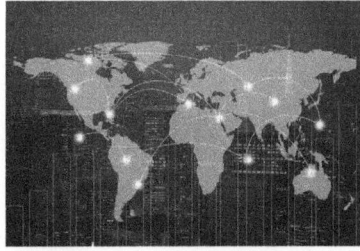

AUTHOR CONTACT PAGE

Prophetess Jackie Harewood
37041 Agnes Webb Avenue
Prairieville, LA 70769

jharewoodla@cox.net
(225) 772-4552

www.ingramcontent.com/pod-product-compliance
Lightning Source LLC
Chambersburg PA
CBHW030924090426
42737CB00007B/307